Andrew Brodie Basics

LET'S DO GRAMMAR

FOR AGES 10-11

- Over 50 activities
- Regular progress tests
- Matched to the National Curriculum

with over **100** reward stickers

Andrew Brodie
An imprint of Bloomsbury Publishing Plc

50 Bedford Square
London
WC1B 3DP
UK

1385 Broadway
New York
NY 10018
USA

www.bloomsbury.com

ANDREW BRODIE is a trademark of Bloomsbury Publishing Plc

First published in Great Britain 2017

ISBN
PB: 978-1-4729-4082-7
ePDF: 978-1-4729-4071-1

2 4 6 8 10 9 7 5 3 1

Designed and typeset by Marcus Duck Design
Printed and bound in China by Leo Paper Products

This book is produced using paper that is made from wood grown in managed, sustainable forests. It is natural, renewable and recyclable. The logging and manufacturing processes conform to the environmental regulations of the country of origin.

To find out more about our authors and books visit www.bloomsbury.com. Here you will find extracts, author interviews, details of forthcoming events and the option to sign up for our newsletters.

BLOOMSBURY

Notes for parents

What's in this book

This is the sixth in the series of *Andrew Brodie Basics: Let's Do Grammar* books. Each book features a clearly structured approach to developing and improving children's knowledge and use of grammar in their reading and writing as well as in their oral communication.

The National Curriculum states that children in Year 6 should know appropriate terminology in relation to grammar and punctuation, including the following:
- singular, plural, suffix, prefix, noun, noun phrase, adjective, verb, adverb, compound, fronted adverbial, conjunction, clause, subordinate clause, co-ordination, subordination, preposition, determiner, modal verb, relative pronoun, relative clause, synonym, antonym, active, passive, subject, object
- sentence, statement, question, exclamation*, command, direct speech, paragraph, cohesion, ambiguity
- present tense, present perfect tense, past tense, present progressive, past progressive, active and passive voice
- punctuation: capital letter, full stop, question mark, exclamation mark, apostrophe, speech marks, inverted commas, parenthesis, bracket, dash, ellipsis, semi-colon, colon, bullet points, hyphens to avoid ambiguity.

*Note that in 2016 the Government stated that, in tests, pupils will only gain marks for exclamations that begin with 'what' or 'how'.

Children will continue learning to:
- use relative clauses, special types of subordinate clauses that modify nouns, beginning with *who, which, where, when, whose, that*
- indicate degrees of possibility using adverbs (e.g. *perhaps, surely*) or modal verbs (e.g. *might, should, will, must*)
- use devices to build cohesion within a paragraph (e.g. *then, after that, this, firstly*)
- link ideas across paragraphs using adverbials of time, place and number, or choice of tense (e.g. *later, nearby, secondly, he had seen her before*) and developing this further through repetition of a word or phrase, the use of adverbials and the use of ellipsis
- use brackets, dashes or commas to indicate parenthesis
- use commas to clarify meaning or avoid ambiguity.

As they approach the end of Year 6, pupils will be tested on grammar as part of their English Standard Attainment Tests. This book contains a wide range of materials designed to provide excellent practice for the tests.

How you can help

Make sure your child is ready for their grammar practice and help them to enjoy the activities in this book. If necessary, read through each activity out loud, discussing it so that your child really understands what the writing means.

The answer section at the end of this book can be a useful teaching tool: ask your child to compare their responses to the ones shown. Their answers may not be identical but should include similar information. If your child has made mistakes, help them to learn from them. Remember that the speed at which your child progresses will vary from topic to topic.

Most importantly, enjoy the experience of working with your child and sharing the excitement of learning together.

Look out for...

Pedro the Panda, who will help your child understand what to focus on when working through the activities.

Brodie's Brain Boosters, which feature quick extra activities designed to make your child think, using the skills and knowledge they already have. Can they talk about their experiences using appropriate and interesting vocabulary?

Contents

Commas

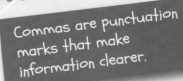
Commas are punctuation marks that make information clearer.

Commas are often used in lists. Look at the sentences below.

We could choose from tea, coffee or hot chocolate.

This is a list of three drinks but only one comma is needed.

There were robins, sparrows, blackbirds and starlings on the lawn.

This is a list of four types of bird but only two commas are used.

Add commas in the correct places in the sentence below.

We needed bricks tiles windows and doors to build the shed.

Look at this sentence.

After tea fruit and biscuits are still available.

The sentence needs at least one comma.

Look:

After tea, fruit and biscuits are still available.

This sentence shows that it is possible to have fruit and biscuits after having tea.

Now look:

After, tea, fruit and biscuits are still available.

This sentence shows that tea and fruit and biscuits are all available after something else, but we don't know what that is.

Insert a comma in the sentence below to make it clear that only Jess and Isla went back home.

Once they had left Jeff Jess and Isla went back home.

Insert two commas in the sentence below to make it clear that all three people went back home.

Once they had left Jeff Jess and Isla went back home.

Brodie's Brain Booster

Look on the first page of a novel. How many commas can you see? Look at the first sentence that contains a comma: is that comma doing an important job?

Subordinate clauses

Every sentence includes a main clause.

Look at these key facts:

- **A clause is a phrase that contains a verb**

- **Every sentence includes a main clause**

- **A main clause could stand on its own as a simple sentence**

- **A sentence may also have one or more subordinate clauses**

- **A subordinate clause may give extra information but could not stand on its own as a simple sentence**

- **The subordinate clause may be at the start, the end or in the middle of a sentence.**

Underline the subordinate clause in each sentence below.

I love running, although I'm not very fast.

Although it's a bit early, would you like to start the work?

If it rings, would you answer the telephone?

Tick one box in each row to show whether the underlined clause is a main clause or a subordinate clause.

Sentence	Main clause	Subordinate clause
My house, <u>which has three bedrooms</u>, was built in 2012.		
<u>Although it's raining</u>, we can still go for a long walk.		
We may win the competition <u>if we are lucky</u>.		
<u>After we've had tea</u>, we'll take the dog for a walk.		

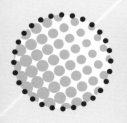

Brodie's Brain Booster

Look at the first page of a novel. Can you find a sentence that contains a subordinate clause? Can you find a sentence that contains more than one subordinate clause? Clue: Find the main clause, which is the one that could be written on its own and would still make sense.

Separating clauses

Commas are often used to separate clauses.

Look at these sentences.

After the race, everyone felt like celebrating.

Before we could go on holiday, we had to check that our passports were still valid.

The subordinate clauses are separated from the main clauses by using commas.

One comma is missing from each sentence below. Write a comma in the correct place.

Smiling happily the girl collected her prize.

Walking slowly we were careful not to frighten the birds.

Despite being late we still managed to find good seats.

The boy reached the top of the tree although it was very tall.

Look at this sentence:

The risotto that I ate was very tasty.

I could have just said: The risotto was very tasty.

The clause that I ate **is called a subordinate clause because it is not as important as the main clause** the risotto was very tasty**. Notice that no commas were necessary.**

Write a sentence that contains a subordinate clause.

_____

_____

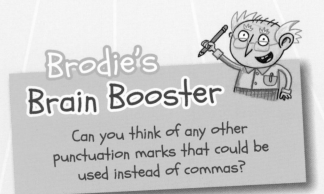

Brodie's
Brain Booster

Can you think of any other punctuation marks that could be used instead of commas?

Bracketing commas

Commas often separate out information that is not essential.

The dog, a small poodle, kept yapping and jumping up.

In this sentence, the extra information is written between commas because it's not important. The breed of dog is irrelevant. Commas used like this are called bracketing commas. The phrase between the commas is known as a parenthesis. The plural of parenthesis is parentheses.

Rewrite the sentences below, inserting commas to separate out the parentheses.

The dogs both of them were barking up the wrong tree.

_____

Dave my dad's friend is very good at woodwork.

_____

My garden which is quite small is full of bright flowers.

_____

Sometimes we use brackets instead of commas.

The dog (a small poodle) kept yapping and jumping up.

Sometimes we use dashes instead of commas or brackets.

The dog – a small poodle – kept yapping and jumping up.

Sometimes a single dash is used to emphasise the end of a sentence. Look at this example.

The food, the games, the ice-cream – this is why I love parties.

Compose your own sentence that uses a single dash.

_____

_____

Brodie's Brain Booster

Look in a novel. Can you find any brackets or dashes?

Relative clauses

The bike that I rode was very comfortable.

Look at Pedro the panda's sentence:

The bike that I rode was very comfortable.

The clause that I rode **is called a** subordinate clause **because it is not as important as the main clause** the bike was very comfortable. **It is also a** relative clause, **which is a special type of subordinate clause. A relative clause modifies a noun and often includes** who, which, where, when, whose **or** that.

Underline the relative clauses in the sentences below.

The picture that is above the fireplace shows a storm at sea.

I asked my friends who were running too fast to slow down a bit.

The slide where the swings used to be is very popular with small children.

Rewrite the sentences below adding a relative clause to each one. Don't forget that a clause must include a verb. Don't forget that a relative clause gives information about a noun.

The bonfire gave out a lot of heat.

_____

_____

The firework display lasted for over half an hour.

_____

_____

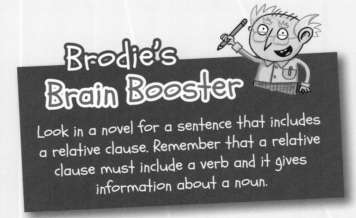

Brodie's Brain Booster

Look in a novel for a sentence that includes a relative clause. Remember that a relative clause must include a verb and it gives information about a noun.

Conjunctions

A conjunction links two words, phrases or clauses together.

There are two main types of conjunction:

- **co-ordinating** conjunctions link two words, phrases or clauses together as an equal pair

- **subordinating** conjunctions introduce a subordinate clause. (Look back at page 5, if you need to, to revise subordinate clauses.)

Here are some words that can work as conjunctions:

| and | when | but | because | if | until | so | then | yet | as | or | before |

Underline the conjunction in each sentence below. Decide whether the conjunction is co-ordinating or subordinating and write your choice in the box.

I'd like to go to the party but I'm going to visit my nan that evening.

_____

The choir had no words to follow, yet they knew the lyrics perfectly.

_____

Keep writing the story until the bell rings for break time.

_____

We'll have to wait for a while as we're early.

_____

Write conjunctions from the box in the correct places in the sentence below. Use each conjunction once.

| or | but | and |

I can carry my towel _____ the picnic _____ the deckchair _____ I can't manage all of them.

Brodie's **Brain Booster**

Some words, like **before**, can be used as conjunctions, adverbs or prepositions.

What is the name of the punctuation marks on either side of the words 'which I had for my birthday' in the sentence below?

The scooter (which I had for my birthday) was silver coloured.

_____

Name at least one other punctuation mark that could be used correctly in the same place.

_____

Tick one box in each row to show whether the commas are used correctly in the sentence.

Sentence	Commas used correctly	Commas used incorrectly
Jess, who has been training hard, is running in lots of races at the moment.		
Jess loves running, swimming, dancing and drama.		
Jess is getting faster, all the time and will soon be winning lots of races.		
Jess takes lots of clothes and equipment such as trainers, tennis rackets, hockey, sticks, and helmets when she goes to the sports centre.		

Use suitable conjunctions to join these pairs of simple sentences.

The headteacher visited our classroom. She was showing some parents around the school.

_____

The car is really dirty. There is so much mud on the road.

_____

Determiners

Determiners are usually very short words.

Three very special determiners are the a and an. These are called articles: the is the determiner that goes before known nouns and it is called the definite article; a and an are the determiners that go before unknown nouns and are called the indefinite articles.

Look at these two sentences:

We need to go across the bridge to get to Wales.

We need to go across a bridge to get to the South Bank.

In the first sentence above, we are referring to a particular bridge. We call it a known bridge because we know which bridge we are going to use.

In the second sentence, the bridge we are going to use is unknown – we don't mind which bridge we use.

Write the correct determiners in the sentence below.

We crossed _____ first bridge then saw_____ sign telling us to take _____ alternative route.

We use the indefinite article an in front of nouns that start with a vowel letter.

We use the indefinite article a in front of nouns that start with a consonant letter.

Write a or an in front of the nouns below.

_____	conjunction	_____	adverb
_____	adjective	_____	article
_____	clause	_____	preposition
_____	noun	_____	pronoun
_____	verb		

We can write the definite article the in front of any noun.

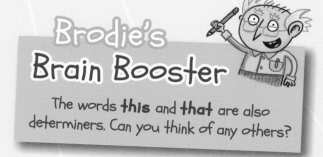

Brodie's
Brain Booster

The words **this** and **that** are also determiners. Can you think of any others?

11

Standard English

All of us speak informally sometimes.

When we are chatting to our friends, we often use informal language and we may use slang words. When we talk in formal situations or when we are writing we usually use Standard English.

Read the sentences below. One of them is written in Standard English. Write a tick next to that one.

My friend done some really good handstands.

I am hoping to get a new bike for my birthday.

We was watching the sports channel.

I were thinking about getting a new bike.

How come all the chocolate has gone?

Now rewrite the other four sentences changing them to Standard English, altering words where necessary.

_____

_____

_____

_____

Brodie's Brain Booster

Using a dictionary, find the difference between slang and dialect. Do you know of any words belonging to a particular dialect?

Sentence types

There are four types of sentence.

Draw a line to match each sentence to its correct function. Use each sentence and each function box only once.

The grass has grown so we can play on the field.

What games should we play on the field?

Fetch the ball so we can play tennis.

What a great day for playing on the field!

exclamation

statement

question

command

Write the correct punctuation mark at the end of each sentence below. You can use full stops, question marks or exclamation marks.

What a difficult journey that was

Did you have a difficult journey

You must go on a long journey

The journey will be long and difficult but it will be worth it

Write one of each type of sentence.

_____

_____

_____

_____

Brodie's Brain Booster

An exclamation is a sudden cry of surprise, anger, fear, pain, excitement or joy and is marked by an exclamation mark. Exclamation sentences also end with exclamation marks.

Nouns and verbs

A noun is a naming word: it gives the name of a person, an animal, a place, an idea or a thing.

Look at this sentence: The baby's laughter amused the teenagers.

This sentence has three nouns: baby, laughter and teenagers. It's easy to tell that baby and teenagers are nouns but it's harder to tell that laughter is a noun.

One way of testing whether a word is a noun is to try putting a determiner (a, an or the) in front of it: if it sounds right with one or more of them then it's likely to be a noun.

- A laughter doesn't sound right.
- An laughter doesn't sound right.
- The laughter does sound right. So, laughter is a noun.

A verb is a word that either shows doing some form of action (swims, drinks, swimming, drinking, swam, drank) or shows a state of being (am, is, was, are, were).

Look at this sentence again: The baby's laughter amused the teenagers.

This sentence contains one verb: amused. It's easy to tell that amused is the verb because it is what the laughter is doing to the teenagers.

Write a sentence using the word run as a verb. Do not change the word. Use correct punctuation.

_____

Write a sentence using the word run as a noun. Do not change the word. Use correct punctuation.

_____

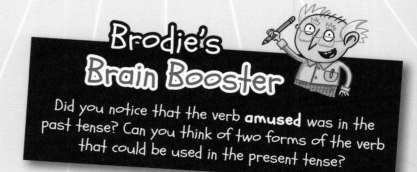

Brodie's Brain Booster

Did you notice that the verb **amused** was in the past tense? Can you think of two forms of the verb that could be used in the present tense?

The subject of a sentence

The subject of a sentence:

- **is the person or thing that is** doing **or** being **something**

- **can be a** noun, noun phrase **or** pronoun

- **is normally** just before the verb **in most sentences**

- **is sometimes** after the verb in a question.

Usually, the big clue in finding the subject is to look just before the verb.

Underline the subject in each sentence below.

Mum drove along the muddy track very slowly.

The lorry swerved to avoid the bike.

The large polar bear ran quickly over the ice.

They enjoyed the show enormously.

Sometimes, there is more than one subject in a sentence.

Underline the subjects in each sentence below.

Jess walked to school but Isla rode to school on her bike.

The pilot flew the plane skilfully and it landed smoothly.

Yesterday we went to our friends' house, but today they are coming to ours.

The days are getting colder so we are dressing warmly.

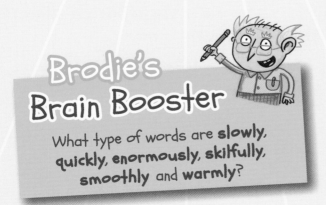

Brodie's Brain Booster

What type of words are **slowly, quickly, enormously, skilfully, smoothly** and **warmly**?

The object of a sentence

Most sentences have an object.

The subject does something. The verb tells us what the subject does. The object is who or what it was done to.

Look at this sentence:

The pilot flew the plane skilfully.

The **subject** of the sentence is pilot, because he was the one doing something.

The verb is flew, because it says what the pilot was doing.

The object is the plane because that is what the pilot was doing something to.

The object:

- is usually a noun but it can also be a pronoun or a noun phrase
- comes straight after the verb
- shows what the verb is acting upon.

Underline the subject and circle the object in each sentence below.

Mum reversed the car.

The children visited the museum.

Our teacher praised us.

Look at this sentence:

My friend has invited my sister and me to the party.

The subject of the sentence is my friend because she or he did something.

The verb is invited because it says what the friend did.

The object is my sister and me because the friend invited both of them. This is called a compound object because there is more than one.

Underline the subject and circle the compound object in each sentence below.

Mum was pleased with my brother and me.

The dog ran after the cat and the mouse.

Brodie's Brain Booster

Look in a novel. Can you find a sentence containing a compound object?

Draw lines to match the sentences to the correct determiner. Use each determiner once.

Sentence   Determiner

I picked _____ apple off the tree.

the

After I'd eaten the apple, I picked _____ plum.

an

There are lots of fruit trees in _____ orchard.

a

Rearrange the words in the statement below to make it a question. Do not add or remove any words. Don't forget the correct punctuation.

Statement: We are going to the shops later.

Question: _____

Rearrange the words in the question below to make it a statement. Do not add or remove any words. Don't forget the correct punctuation.

Question: Is there a plum in the fruit bowl?

Statement: _____

Write a sentence using the word catch as a verb. Do not change the word. Use correct punctuation.

_____

Write a sentence using the word catch as a noun. Do not change the word. Use correct punctuation.

_____

Underline the subject and circle the object in the sentence below.

The little girl frightened the pigeon.

Antonyms and synonyms

Is the weather too hot or too cold?

Two words are **antonyms** if they mean **opposite things to each other**.

We say that hot is the opposite of cold, so the antonym of hot is cold and the antonym of cold is hot.

Write a possible antonym for each word below. One word appears twice because it has more than one antonym, depending on its meaning.

tall _____   bright _____

narrow _____   high _____

wet _____   under _____

light _____   back _____

light _____   long _____

big _____   kind _____

Two words are **synonyms** if they mean the **same thing or have similar meanings**.

We say that talk means roughly the same thing as speak, so a synonym of talk is speak and a synonym of speak is talk.

Write a possible synonym for each word below.

cry _____   scarlet _____

jog _____   cap _____

build _____   important _____

slice _____   funny _____

fall _____   intelligent _____

Brodie's Brain Booster

Can you give an antonym and a synonym for the word **simple**?

Adjectives

Adjectives modify nouns or pronouns. They describe what they are like: for example, what colour they are, what size they are and how many of them there are.

Look at this sentence:

A large lorry passed the small car.

There are two nouns in the sentence: lorry, car.

There are two adjectives in the sentence: large, small.

Write suitable adjectives in the sentence below.

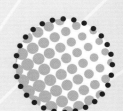

The _____ boat sailed across the _____ sea.

Look at this sentence:

Forty, large, pink flamingoes landed at the edge of the lake.

There are three nouns in the sentence: flamingoes, edge, lake.

There are three adjectives in the sentence but they are all referring to only one noun, flamingoes. **Notice the use of commas to separate the adjectives.**

Write suitable adjectives in the sentence below.

I saw _____ , _____ , _____ cars parked in a row.

Some adjectives can be made from other words by adding suffixes.

Draw lines to match the words to the suffixes to make adjectives.

Word	Suffix
care	ish
child	able
break	ful

Use one of the adjectives in a sentence.

_____

_____

Adjectives and adverbs

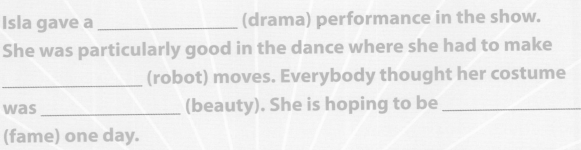

Complete the passage with adjectives derived from the nouns in brackets.

Isla gave a _____ (drama) performance in the show.
She was particularly good in the dance where she had to make
_____ (robot) moves. Everybody thought her costume
was _____ (beauty). She is hoping to be _____
(fame) one day.

An adverb can describe or modify a verb, an adjective or even another adverb.

Look at these sentences:

I rode my bike quickly.

The ride was really exciting.

I rode my bike very quickly.

In the first sentence the adverb quickly describes the verb rode. It says how I rode my bike.

In the second sentence the adverb really modifies the adjective exciting.

In the third sentence the adverb very modifies the adverb quickly.

Circle the four adverbs in the sentence below.

The dancer moved incredibly fast and performed absolutely brilliantly.

Complete each sentence with an appropriate adverb.

Mum climbed the ladder _____.

She ran _____ in the race.

He settled down to sleep _____.

Brodie's
Brain Booster

Look at the first page of a novel.
Can you find any adverbs?

Adverbs

I chewed crunchily on my bamboo.

Lots of adverbs can be made by adding the suffix **ly** to another word.

Use the suffix **ly** to change each of these adjectives to adverbs. You may need to make other changes too.

thorough _____

careful _____

understandable _____

magic _____

necessary _____

separate _____

automatic _____

argumentative _____

Use one of the adverbs in a sentence.

_____

_____

Complete the passage with adverbs derived from the nouns in brackets.

Isla performed _____ (drama) in the show. She was particularly good in the dance where she had to move _____ (robot). Everybody thought her costume was _____ (beauty) made. At the end of the show, the audience clapped _____ (enthusiasm). Isla bowed _____ (pride).

Brodie's **Brain Booster**

Can you think of two adverbs that do not end in **ly**?

Adverbials

A phrase is a group of words that are grammatically connected.

A group of words can work like an adverb in an **adverbial clause** or an **adverbial phrase**. An adverbial is a clause or phrase that is used to add information to a verb or another clause.

Look at this sentence:

I'll eat some bamboo after I've read this page.

The clause after I've read this page **is an adverbial that answers the question when will I eat?**

Now this sentence:

We need to stop work because it's getting late.

The clause because it's getting late **is an adverbial that answers the question why will we stop work?**

Look at this sentence:

I can collect the new bike from the back of the shop.

The phrase from the back of the shop **is an adverbial that answers the question where will I get the bike?**

Add an adverbial to the end of each of these sentences:

I'll clean my teeth _____.

The train is arriving late _____.

We'll get off the train _____.

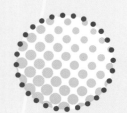

Brodie's Brain Booster

Look in a novel. Can you find any adverbials?

Fronted adverbials

Remember, an adverbial is a clause or phrase that is used to add information to a verb or another clause. Look at the sentences below. The adverbials are shown.

I'm going to have lunch after I've finished my maths.

The old city can be found on the other side of the mountain.

Look at how these sentences can be rewritten in a different order.

After I've finished my maths, I'm going to have lunch.

On the other side of the mountain, the old city can be found.

Did you notice that the adverbials have been moved to the front and separated from the main clause by a comma? We call these fronted adverbials.

Rewrite the sentences below so that they have fronted adverbials. Don't forget to include a comma in each sentence.

We can collect the costumes for the show after we've had tea.

_____

We need to get changed into our swimsuits before we can go for a swim.

_____

There are three lorries parked on the far side of the car park.

_____

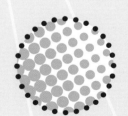

Brodie's Brain Booster

Write a sentence of your own using a fronted adverbial.

Write a definition of the word antonym:

_____

Write one word that is an antonym of mean: _____

Write a definition of the word synonym:

_____

Write one word that is a synonym of shut: _____

Add an adverbial to the end of each of these sentences:

We can run round the track _____.

The classroom needs to be tidied _____.

Write a fronted adverbial for each of these sentences:

_____ I'm going to have something to eat.

_____ you will find your present.

Complete the passage with adverbs or adjectives derived from the words in brackets.

The headteacher said she was _____ (pride) of all of us for the work we had done. She said she was _____ (particular) pleased that everybody had worked as part of a team. She said she hoped we would enjoy our _____ (length) summer holidays and would return _____ (enthusiasm) in September.

Present tense

The past has gone, the present is now, the future is still to come.

Don't forget, a verb is a doing or being word.

Present tense doing words:

Singular forms
I do
you do
she does, he does, it does

I catch
you catch
she catches, he catches, it catches

Plural forms
we do
you do
they do

we catch
you catch
they catch

Write the present tense forms of the word chase.

_____ _____

_____ _____

Present tense being:

Singular forms
I am
you are
she is, he is, it is

Plural forms
we are
you are
they are

We often use the present participle form of a verb, ending with ing; for example, running, walking, racing, strolling, shouting, gardening.

We could say I am running. The verb running is the present participle. It is accompanied by the auxiliary verb am. Together, am and running form the present progressive form of the verb run.

Here are the present progressive forms of the verb catch:

Singular forms
I am catching
you are   catching
she is, he is, it is catching

Plural forms
we are catching
you are catching
they are catching

Write a sentence containing the present progressive form of the verb buy.

_____

_____

25

Past tense

The past is behind me.

If something has already happened we use the past tense.
Here is the simple past tense of the verb look:

look ⟶ looked

That was easy, but look at the simple past tense of the verb catch:

catch ⟶ caught

Write the simple past tense of each verb below. If you are not sure, try each word in a present tense and a past tense sentence.

happen ⟶ _____

want ⟶ _____

knock ⟶ _____

mix ⟶ _____

know ⟶ _____

fly ⟶ _____

drink ⟶ _____

think ⟶ _____

blink ⟶ _____

speak ⟶ _____

sneak ⟶ _____

go ⟶ _____

Complete each sentence below, using the simple past tense of the verb shown in the box.

climb   see

When we had _____ the hill, we _____ a beautiful view.

buy   go

I _____ a bar of chocolate when I _____ to the shop.

Circle the two words that show the tense of the sentence below.

We came home after we watched the race.

Past progressive

Remember, the progressive form of the verb generally shows events in progress.

Here are the past progressive forms of the verb lift:

Singular forms
I was lifting
you were lifting
she was, he was, it was lifting

Plural forms
we were lifting
you were lifting
they were lifting

Write a sentence containing the past progressive form of the verb enjoy.

_____

_____

Complete this chart for the verb carry.

Present	Present progressive	Simple past	Past progressive
I carry	I am carrying	I carried	I was carrying
you carry (singular)			
she/he/it carries			
we carry			
you carry (plural)			
they carry			

Complete this chart for the verb go.

Present	Present progressive	Simple past	Past progressive
I go	I am going	I went	I was going
you go (singular)			
she/he/it goes			
we go			
you go (plural)			
they go			

Brodie's Brain Booster

Look in a novel. Can you find an example of the present progressive or the past progressive?

Active and passive

All the bamboo was eaten by my friend!

We can use verbs in **the active voice** or in **the passive voice.**

With the active voice **the subject** does something.

With the passive voice **something** is done **to the subject.**

My mum made some sandwiches for my lunch.   **This is in the active voice.**

My sandwiches were made by my mum.   **This is in the passive voice.**

Tick one box in each row to show whether the sentence is written in the active voice or the passive voice.

Sentence	Active	Passive
Cars travel very fast on the motorway.		
The motorway is used by many lorries.		
Coaches usually stay in the inside lane.		
Usually, lorries are overtaken by cars.		

Rewrite the sentences below so that they are in the active voice.

The prizes were presented by a famous celebrity.

_____

All the goals were scored by just one girl.

_____

Rewrite the sentences below so that they are in the passive voice.

A herd of cows chased us across the field.

_____

The wind blew the clouds quickly across the sky.

_____

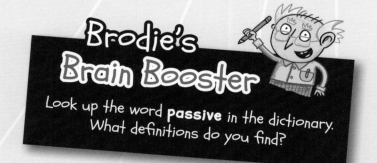

Brodie's
Brain Booster

Look up the word **passive** in the dictionary.
What definitions do you find?

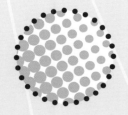

Present perfect

A perfect present would be some bamboo... but this page is about the present perfect.

The **present perfect** tense is created from the present tense of the verb **have** and the **past participle** of a verb. For example:

I have finished my work for today.

You have written a brilliant story.

He has caught a bad cold.

She has been to London several times.

Which sentence uses the present perfect form?

Tick one.

Jess finished her homework very quickly. ☐

Jess has collected a huge number of stamps. ☐

Jess was watching the sports channel. ☐

Jess did the washing up before going out for a run. ☐

Write three sentences in the present perfect form.

_____

_____

_____

_____

_____

_____

Brodie's Brain Booster

Did you know that we refer to three **persons** when we study grammar? The **first person** is the speaker: **I, we**. The **second person** is the hearer: **you**. The **third person** is the person or thing being spoken about: **he, she, it, they**.

Modal verbs

I can tell you about modal verbs: I ought to tell you, and I will tell you.

Modal verbs change the meaning of other verbs.
The main modal verbs are shown in the box below.

MODAL VERBS:

can   could   will   would   shall   should   may   might   must   ought

Write an appropriate modal verb in each gap below.

Mum told me that I _____ finish my homework before going out to play.

I think I _____ to get my homework done quite quickly.

I _____ finish my homework but I _____ not complete it on time.

My sister _____ like to perform on the stage.

I hope I _____ see her when she performs her song.

My mum said that my sister _____ be famous one day.

Write three sentences that each include a modal verb.

_____

_____

_____

_____

_____

Brodie's Brain Booster

Look in a novel. What is the first modal verb that you find?

Tick one box in each row to show if the sentence is in the present progressive or the past progressive.

Sentence	Present progressive	Past progressive
Jess is running in lots of races at the moment.		
Jess was running in a race at the weekend.		
Jess is getting faster all the time.		

Write an appropriate modal verb in each gap below.

The giraffe _____ be able to reach the leaves at the top of the tree.

I _____ go to sleep after I have read three more pages of my book.

Write a sentence in the present perfect form.

_____

_____

Rewrite the sentence below so that it is in the active voice.

The house was built by two people.

_____

Write a sentence containing the past progressive form of the verb eat.

_____

_____

Circle the two words that show the tense of the sentence below.

The boys bought their tickets then went to London.

31

Prefixes

A prefix can be added to the start of some words to change their meaning.

PREFIX BOX:

anti auto centi circum demi dis extra hyper inter intra kilo mega

milli mono multi photo pre re semi sub super tele trans

Normally, adding a prefix doesn't change the spelling of the word to which it's being added.

Make some new words by adding prefixes to the words below.

market ➡️ _____ _____

national ➡️ _____ _____

metre ➡️ _____ _____

_____ _____

graph ➡️ _____ _____

_____ _____

gram ➡️ _____ _____

_____ _____

_____

Circle the correct word to explain how the prefix changes the meaning of the sentence in each of the examples below.

The pilot reported that the plane would be flying at subsonic speeds.

This means that the plane was flying at speeds *above/below* **the speed of sound.**

The pilot reported that the plane would be flying at supersonic speeds.

This means that the plane was flying at speeds *above/below* **the speed of sound.**

Brodie's Brain Booster
Can you make new words from the words listed above by adding a suffix instead of a prefix?

Prepositions

Pedro the panda likes to sleep up in the branches of a tree.

The words **up** and **in** are both **prepositions**. Prepositions are usually written before nouns. They often link that noun to another word in the sentence. They often describe locations or time.

Some words, like **before**, can be used as conjunctions, adverbs or prepositions.

Conjunctions connect two clauses together: I'm going to have tea **before** I go swimming.

Adverbs often modify verbs: I've been to France once **before**.

Prepositions are followed by nouns: Pedro the panda likes to sleep **before** lunch.

PREPOSITION BOX:

in   under   below   between   up   down   towards

to   on   above   before   after   into

Here are some sentences. Choose a preposition to fill each gap.

I need to go to the shops _____ the party.

We are headed _____ the High Street.

The tile slipped _____ the roof and _____ the gutter.

The drone hovered _____ the garden.

Write a sentence that includes at least one preposition.

_____

_____

Brodie's Brain Booster

Look in a novel. Can you find any prepositions on the first page?

33

Pronouns

We often use pronouns in place of nouns.

Here are some pronouns we can use in place of nouns or proper nouns:

it   he   she   I   you   we   they   me   us   them   him   her

Replace the underlined word or words in each sentence below with an appropriate pronoun.

Jess watched television for a while, then <u>Jess</u> did her homework. _____

There was a lot of homework to do and Jess took a long time over <u>her homework</u>.

_____

Possessive pronouns are used to show who owns something:

my   your   her   his   hers   mine   our   ours   yours   their   theirs   its

Choose the correct possessive pronoun for each gap. The first two are done for you.

Our grandmother gave me the book. This is my book. The book is mine.

Our grandmother gave you a book. This is _____ book. The book is _____ .

Our grandmother gave Amy a book. This is _____ book. The book is _____ .

Our grandmother gave Austin a book. This is _____ book. The book is

_____ .

Our grandmother gave all her grandchildren some books. These are

_____ books. The books are _____ .

Our grandmother gave books to all of us. These are _____ books.

The books are _____ .

Write out the pairs of pronouns you have written. The first pair has been written for you.

_____*your*_____   _____*yours*_____   _____   _____

_____   _____   _____   _____

_____   _____

In one of the pairs, both of the words are identical. What are they?

_____   _____

 # Colons

A colon is made from two dots.

A colon can be used to:

- **introduce a** quotation

- **introduce a** list**, possibly arranged as** bullet points

- separate clauses**, especially where the** second clause explains **or illustrates the first.**

Did you notice that the bulleted list above was introduced by a colon? Look at the next sentence, which also introduces a list.

We found what we needed to take to the beach: a wind-break, some towels, beach games, a picnic and our swimming things.

Write a sentence that includes a colon to introduce a list.

_____

_____

_____

Which sentence below uses the colon correctly? **Tick one**

We had lots to eat some sandwiches: some pies crisps and tomatoes. ☐

We had lots to eat some: sandwiches, some pies, crisps and tomatoes. ☐

We had lots to eat: some sandwiches, some pies, crisps and tomatoes. ☐

We had lots: to eat some sandwiches, some pies, crisps and tomatoes. ☐

 Brodie's Brain Booster

Look in a newspaper or magazine. Can you find a colon?

Semi-colons

The **semi-colon** is placed between two independent clauses that could be separate sentences but just seem to work better in one sentence. Some people use a **dash** for the same purpose.

Write a semi-colon in the correct place in each sentence below.

My friend is coming for a sleepover we're not expecting to get much sleep.

We're going to have a great party lots of people are coming.

The weather is beautiful today there is so much sunshine.

She is really pleased with herself the story she wrote is brilliant.

Look again at the sentences above. Do you think that any of them could have been better with a colon instead of a semi-colon? Choose two of them to rewrite with a colon.

_____

_____

_____

Just like with commas, you can decide whether a semi-colon is needed in a sentence. Sometimes a comma may be better, or a conjunction, or perhaps it would be better to use two sentences. Rewrite the sentence below in the way that you think is best.

Yesterday we visited the local museum we saw lots of interesting things.

_____

_____

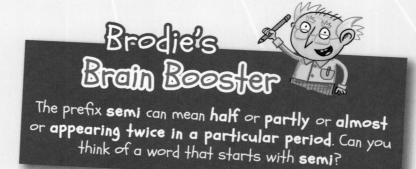

Brodie's Brain Booster

The prefix **semi** can mean **half** or **partly** or **almost** or **appearing twice in a particular period**. Can you think of a word that starts with **semi**?

Hyphens

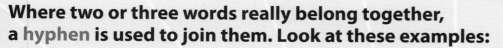

A hyphen looks a bit like a dash but it has a different job.

Where two or three words really belong together, a **hyphen** is used to join them. Look at these examples:

The eleven-year-old girls are singing together in the show tonight.

He is delighted that his mother-in-law is coming to stay for a fortnight.

My mum likes to buy sugar-free drinks.

My teacher is never bad-tempered.

I was thrilled to see a well-known celebrity.

Hyphens can help to remove ambiguity in sentences. Look again at the first sentence above, which is rewritten here without the hyphens:

The eleven year old girls are singing together in the show tonight.

This sentence could mean that eleven girls who are all one year old are singing in the show – it would be quite a show!

Which sentence below uses the hyphen correctly?   **Tick one**

My sport-mad sister is always watching football matches on TV.   ☐

My sport-mad-sister is always watching football matches on TV.   ☐

My sport mad-sister is always watching football matches on TV.   ☐

Hyphens can also be used to join prefixes to other words when necessary. Hyphens can be really useful for words like re-cover as opposed to recover. The first example refers to putting a new cover on something, whereas the second means something completely different – to get well again!

Brodie's
Brain Booster

Did you know that the word **co-ordinate** can also be spelled without a hyphen?

Replace the underlined word or words in each sentence below with the correct possessive pronoun.

The ball belongs to <u>you</u>. The ball is _____.

These shoes belong to <u>my sister</u>. These shoes are _____.

The bow and arrow belong to <u>me</u>. The bow and arrow are _____.

The two cars are owned by <u>my grandparents</u>. The two cars are _____.

Circle all the prepositions in the sentence below.

The bags are in the cupboard under the stairs below the coats.

Rewrite the sentence below, inserting hyphens in the correct places.

My sister in law has decided to recover the old worn out sofa.

_____

Write a semi-colon in the correct place in each sentence below.

The weather forecast is fine for tomorrow we'll be able to go to the beach.

The robot is very impressive it has twenty-four different functions.

Rewrite the sentence below, punctuating it correctly.

mum gave me the shopping list milk bread beans butter and rice

_____

38

Apostrophes

I could've eaten lots more bamboo.

We often merge words together to make them easier to say. To do this, we miss letters out and replace them with an apostrophe. We call the process contraction. Here are some examples:

it is ➡ it's   can not ➡ can't

I have ➡ I've   will not ➡ won't

Write the contracted version of these pairs of words:

we are _____   should not _____

they have _____   does not _____

was not _____   did not _____

could have _____   we will _____

should have _____   they will _____

would have _____   they are _____

must have _____   I have _____

Be careful! Some people write could of or must of when they should have written could've or must've, or could have or must have: just because a word sounds like of it doesn't mean it is! Here's a clue: temporarily remove the modal verb (must or could, for example) from your sentence and decide whether you need of or have. Look at Pedro the panda's example:

I could've eaten lots more bamboo. ➡ I have eaten lots more bamboo.

We can see that have is the correct word. 'I of eaten lots more bamboo' does not make sense.

Rewrite the sentence below, contracting two pairs of words by using apostrophes.

I could have written a bit more if I had had more time.

_____

Replace the underlined words with their expanded forms.

They've been swimming so they're soaking wet.

_____

Ownership

I'm eating my bamboo in my tree.

The word **my** is a possessive pronoun. Write four more possessive pronouns.

_____   _____   _____

We can also show possession by using possessive apostrophes:

This is Tariq's bike. The bike is his.

Ownership shown by a possessive apostrophe.

Ownership shown by a possessive pronoun.

Rewrite the sentences below, inserting possessive apostrophes where appropriate.

Austin was playing cards with Maxs friends.

_____

The ships hull was coated in barnacles.

_____

We chased Amys rabbit round Nicks garden but it escaped and went into the neighbours vegetable garden.

_____

_____

Everyone thought the familys car had caught fire when smoke started pouring out of its engine.

_____

_____

Brodie's Brain Booster

Lots of people use apostrophes in the wrong places. Apostrophes should only be used where letters have been missed out or to show possession. Apostrophes should never be used to make plurals.

Apostrophes with plural nouns

Remember, don't use apostrophes to make plural nouns.

The girl's phone is new. The other girls' phones are a bit older.

There is one girl. The apostrophe goes before the letter s.

The word girls is plural. The apostrophe goes after the letter s.

The possessive apostrophe always goes after the owner or owners. When there is one girl there is only one owner so the possessive apostrophe goes straight after the word girl. When there is more than one girl, the possessive apostrophe goes after the word girls.

The possessive apostrophes have been missed out of the sentences below. Rewrite the sentences, using possessive apostrophes correctly.

This is the boys changing room.

_____

This is the girls changing room.

_____

The mens clothes are on the ground floor. (Remember, only put the apostrophe with the owners. Think about who the clothes are for.)

_____

The womens clothes are on the first floor.

_____

The parents room is at the opposite end of the house to the childrens rooms.

_____

_____

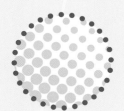

Brodie's Brain Booster

Look at the first five pages of a novel. Can you find any possessive apostrophes?

Inverted commas

Inverted commas are sometimes called speech marks.

Read the unpunctuated text below.

do you want to come over to my place asked tariq we could play football and mum says shell get your favourite tea that would be great replied jasdeep smiling do you think there will be ice cream im sure there will be said tariq

Now read the same text, this time with punctuation.

"Do you want to come over to my place?" asked Tariq. "We could play football and mum says she'll get your favourite tea."

"That would be great!" replied Jasdeep, smiling, "do you think there will be ice cream?"

"I'm sure there will be," said Tariq.

Note: in some books, single speech marks are used instead of double speech marks. Look carefully at how the speech marks are used:

- the words that Tariq and Jasdeep spoke are written between the speech marks
- there is a comma, a question mark, a full stop or an exclamation mark before the closing speech marks
- speech verbs, such as said, replied, cried or asked, are usually written to show who is speaking
- a new line is started when there is a change of speaker.

Rewrite the following short conversation, punctuating it carefully. Use double speech marks, not single speech marks, as they are normally used in handwritten dialogue.

can you tell me the way to the railway station asked the man

its not far away i replied grinning at the man

so where is it he asked again

youre standing right in front of it i exclaimed

_____

_____

_____

_____

Dialogue

A written conversation is called a dialogue.

Read the text below carefully then rewrite it as correctly punctuated dialogue. Don't forget the rules for punctuating speech:

- **the inverted commas (speech marks) are written each side of the actual words spoken**

- **we often have a speech verb such as asked, replied, said, cried, shouted, responded, written with the character's name so that we know who is speaking**

- **there is always a full stop, a comma, an exclamation mark or a question mark before the closing speech marks**

- **a new line is started when the speaker changes.**

do you want to go swimming asked kizzy that would be good replied mia where do you want to go the pool or the beach kizzy asked lets go to the beach for a change said mia what a great idea said kizzy enthusiastically

_____

_____

_____

_____

_____

_____

Brodie's Brain Booster

Look at some dialogue in a novel. Is there always a speech verb and a character name? Can you find any speech where there is not? How is it possible to tell who is speaking?

43

Composing a dialogue

I talk a lot to my friends.

Imagine a conversation between you and your mum or between you and a friend. You could be talking about a special event, something you would like to do, how you feel about going to secondary school, your favourite sport, your pet, or anything you choose. Write the dialogue carefully, remembering the rules shown on page 43.

Brodie's Brain Booster

Dialogue with speech marks indicating the exact words spoken by a character is known as direct speech. Sometimes we report what someone has said without using their exact words: 'My friend told me that she had a new bike for her birthday.' This is known as indirect speech or reported speech.

Circle the one word in the text below that contains a possessive apostrophe.

It's a lovely day today so I'm going to collect my boat from Ted's house and sail it on the pond. He's going out this morning but we'll be able to meet up at about two o'clock.

The inverted commas, or speech marks, are missing from the sentence below. Draw them in the correct places.

There will be an opportunity to go on a residential trip, the headteacher   said.

Rewrite the text below, punctuating it correctly.

do you want to go shopping today mum asked thats the last thing in the world i want to do replied ted it would be really good if you could help me said mum oh all right then said ted reluctantly then we could go and get a burger some chips and a milk shake said mum now thats a great idea exclaimed ted

ANSWERS

Use the answers to check your child's progress but also to give prompts and ideas if they are needed. Note that sometimes your child's answer may not match the answer given here but could be just as good!

 p4

We needed bricks, tiles, windows and doors to build the shed.

Once they had left Jeff, Jess and Isla went back home.

Once they had left, Jeff, Jess and Isla went back home.

Brain Booster:

Help your child to consider the roles commas are playing in the text.

 p5

I love running, although I'm not very fast.

Although it's a bit early, would you like to start the work?

If it rings, would you answer the telephone?

Sentence	Main clause	Subordinate clause
My house, which has three bedrooms, was built in 2012.		✓
Although it's raining, we can still go for a long walk.	✓	
We may win the competition if we are lucky.		✓
After we've had tea, we'll take the dog for a walk.		✓

Brain Booster:

Help your child to find subordinate clauses in a novel.

 p6

Smiling happily, the girl collected her prize.

Walking slowly, we were careful not to frighten the birds.

Despite being late, we still managed to find good seats.

The boy reached the top of the tree, although it was very tall.

Check your child's sentences.

Brain Booster:

Your child may suggest brackets or dashes: discuss which punctuation marks are most appropriate.

 p7

The dogs, both of them, were barking up the wrong tree.

Dave, my dad's friend, is very good at woodwork.

My garden, which is quite small, is full of bright flowers.

Check your child's sentence.

Brain Booster:

Help your child to find any brackets or dashes and to understand why they are used.

 p8

The picture that is above the fireplace shows a storm at sea.

I asked my friends who were running too fast to slow down a bit.

The slide where the swings used to be is very popular with small children.

Check your child's sentences.

Brain Booster:

Help your child to find an appropriate sentence.

 p9

but – co-ordinating

yet – co-ordinating

until – subordinating

as – subordinating

I can carry my towel and the picnic or the deck chair but I can't manage all of them.

Progress Test 1:

brackets; dashes or commas

Sentence	Commas used correctly	Commas used incorrectly
Jess, who has been training hard, is running in lots of races at the moment.	✓	
Jess loves running, swimming, dancing and drama.	✓	
Jess is getting faster, all the time and will soon be winning lots of races.		✓
Jess takes lots of clothes and equipment such as trainers, tennis rackets, hockey, sticks, and helmets when she goes to the sports centre.		✓

Possible answers:

The headteacher visited our classroom as she was showing some parents around the school.

The car is really dirty because there is so much mud on the road.

 p11

We crossed the first bridge then saw a sign telling us to take an alternative route.

a conjunction	an adverb
an adjective	an article
a clause	a preposition
a noun	a pronoun
a verb	

Brain Booster:

those these

 p12

I am hoping to get a new bike for my birthday.

My friend did some really good handstands.

We were watching the sports channel.

I was thinking about getting a new bike.

Where's the chocolate?

Brain Booster:

A dialect is a form of speech from a particular region. Slang consists of words or phrases that are very informal.

 p13

The grass has grown so we can play on the field. statement

What games should we play on the field? question

Fetch the ball so we can play tennis. command

What a great day for playing on the field! exclamation

What a difficult journey that was!

Did you have a difficult journey?

You must go on a long journey.

The journey will be long and difficult but it will be worth it.

Check your child's sentences.

 p14

Possible answers: I like to run every Saturday.

I like to go for a run every Saturday.

Brain Booster:

amuse, amuses

 p15

subject: Mum
subject: The lorry
subject: The large polar bear
subject: They

subjects: Jess, Isla
subjects: pilot, plane
subjects: we, they
subjects: days, we

Brain Booster:

adverbs

 p16

subject: mum	**object:** car
subject: children	**object:** museum
subject: teacher	**object:** us
subject: mum	

compound object: my brother and me
subject: dog
compound object: the cat and the mouse

Brain Booster:

Help your child to find a compound object.

Progress Test 2

an

a

the

Are we going to the shops later?

There is a plum in the fruit bowl.

Possible answers: I tried to catch the ball. My friend made a great catch.

subject: the little girl   **object**: pigeon

p18

Possible answers:

short	dull
wide	low
dry	over
dark	front
heavy	short
little	mean
call or weep	red
run or trot	hat
make or construct	special
cut	amusing
drop	clever

Brain Booster:

difficult easy

p19

Possible answers:

The small boat sailed across the choppy sea.

I saw six , red , shiny cars parked in a row.

careful childish breakable

Check your child's sentence.

p20

dramatic, robotic, beautiful, famous.

incredibly fast absolutely brilliantly

Possible answers:

Mum climbed the ladder carefully .

She ran quickly in the race .

He settled down to sleep comfortably .

Brain Booster:

Help your child to find adverbs.

p21

thoroughly

understandably

necessarily

automatically

carefully

magically

separately

argumentatively

Check your child's sentence.

dramatically, robotically, beautifully, enthusiastically, proudly.

Brain Booster:

possible answers: fast, hard

p22

Check your child's sentences.

Brain Booster:

Help your child to find adverbials in the book.

p23

After we've had tea , we can collect the costumes for the show.

Before we can go for a swim , we need to get changed into our swimsuits.

On the far side of the car park , there are three lorries parked.

Brain Booster:

Check your child's sentence.

Progress Test 3

An antonym is a word that means the opposite of another.   mean: kind

A synonym is a word that means the same or nearly the same as another. shut: close

Check your child's sentences.

proud, particularly, long, enthusiastically.

p25

I chase	we chase
you chase	you chase
she chases, he chases, it chases	they chase

Possible answer:

I am buying some sweets right now.

Brain Booster:

Help your child to think about the questions.

p26

happened

wanted

knocked

mixed

knew

flew

drank

thought

blinked

spoke

sneaked

went

climbed, saw

bought, went

Circled: came watched

p27

Sentence containing was enjoying or were enjoying

Present	Present progressive	Simple past	Past progressive
I carry	I am carrying	I carried	I was carrying
you carry (singular)	You are carrying	You carried	You were carrying
she/he/it carries	She/he/it is carrying	She/he/it carried	She/he/it was carrying
we carry	We are carrying	We carried	We were carrying
you carry (plural)	You are carrying	You carried	You were carrying
they carry	They are carrying	They carried	They were carrying

Present	Present progressive	Simple past	Past progressive
I go	I am going	I went	I was going
you go (singular)	You are going	You went	You were going
she/he/it goes	She/he/it is going	She/he/it went	She/he/it was going
we go	We are going	We went	We were going
you go (plural)	You are going	You went	You were going
they go	They are going	They went	They were going

Brain Booster:

Help your child to find an example of the progressive form.

p28

Sentence	Active	Passive
Cars travel very fast on the motorway.	✓	
The motorway is used by many lorries.		✓
Coaches usually stay in the inside lane.	✓	
Usually, lorries are overtaken by cars.		✓

A famous celebrity presented the prizes.

Just one girl scored all the goals.

We were chased across the field by a herd of cows.

The clouds were blown across the sky by the wind.

Brain Booster:

Help your child to find definitions of passive.

p29

Jess has collected a huge number of stamps.

Check your child's sentences.

p30

Possible answers:

should/must

ought

should/could/will/shall/can/would

may/might/will/can/would

would

will/shall/may

may/might/should/would/will/shall

Check your child's sentences.

Brain Booster:

Help your child to find a modal verb.

Sentence	Present progressive	Past progressive
Jess is running in lots of races at the moment.	✓	
Jess was running in a race at the weekend.		✓
Jess is getting faster all the time.	✓	

Possible answers:

should/will/could/may/might

will/might/may/must

Check your child's sentence.

Two people built the house.

Your child's sentence should contain **was eating** or **were eating**.

Circled: bought went

supermarket hypermarket

international multinational

centimetre kilometre millimeter

autograph monograph photograph telegraph

centigram kilogram milligram monogram telegram

below

above

Brain Booster:

Examples: marketable nationally metric graphic

Possible answers: before towards down into above

Check your child's sentence.

Brain Booster:

Help your child to find prepositions.

she, it

your yours

her hers

his his

their theirs

our ours

his

Check that your child's sentence uses the colon correctly.

We had lots to eat: some sandwiches, some pies, crisps and tomatoes.

Brain Booster:

Help your child to find a colon.

My friend is coming for a sleepover; we're not expecting to get much sleep.

We're going to have a great party; lots of people are coming.

The weather is beautiful today; there is so much sunshine.

She is really pleased with herself; the story she wrote is brilliant.

Any two of:

We're going to have a great party: lots of people are coming.

The weather is beautiful today: there is so much sunshine.

She is really pleased with herself: the story she wrote is brilliant.

Any one of:

Yesterday we visited the local museum; we saw lots of interesting things.

Yesterday we visited the local museum. We saw lots of interesting things.

Yesterday we visited the local museum and saw lots of interesting things.

Brain Booster:

Examples include: semicircle semidetached semifinal semiquaver

My sport-mad sister is always watching football matches on TV.

yours

hers

mine

theirs

in, under, below

sister-in-law, re-cover, worn-out

The weather forecast is fine for tomorrow; we'll be able to go to the beach.

The robot is very impressive; it has twenty-four different functions.

Mum gave me the shopping list: milk, bread, beans, butter and rice

we're   shouldn't

they're   doesn't

wasn't   didn't

could've   we'll

should've   they'll

would've   they're

must've   I've

I could've written a bit more if I'd had more time.

They have they are

Any four of: mine, your, yours, his, her, hers, our, ours, their, theirs

Austin was playing cards with Max's friends.

The ship's hull was coated in barnacles.

We chased Amy's rabbit round Nick's garden but it escaped and went into the neighbour's vegetable garden. (Please note that neighbours' would be the correct form if the vegetable garden belongs to more than one neighbour – your child can choose.)

Everyone thought the family's car had caught fire when smoke started pouring out of its engine.

This is the boys' changing room. (The apostrophe goes after boys because the changing room is for the boys not just for one boy.)

This is the girls' changing room.

The men's clothes are on the ground floor. (The apostrophe goes after men because the clothes are for the men.)

The women's clothes are on the first floor.

The parents' room is at the opposite end of the house to the children's rooms. (Answer shown is for two parents but if there is only one, the apostrophe would go before the s.)

Brain Booster:

Help your child to find possessive apostrophes.

"Can you tell me the way to the railway station?" asked the man.

"It's not far away," I replied, grinning at the man.

"So where is it?" he asked again.

"You're standing right in front of it!" I exclaimed.

Brain Booster:

Help your child to find any examples of dialogues in the book.

"Do you want to go swimming?" asked Kizzy.

"That would be good," replied Mia.

"Where do you want to go, the pool or the beach?" Kizzy asked.

"Let's go to the beach for a change," said Mia.

"What a great idea!" said Kizzy enthusiastically.

Brain Booster:

Help your child to find some dialogue and to work out who is speaking. Sometimes a speech verb and character name are not used by a writer if it is obvious who is speaking, although it's not always that obvious!

Check that your child has written an appropriate dialogue, following the 'rules'.

Circled: Ted's

"There will be an opportunity to go on a residential trip," the headteacher said.

"Do you want to go shopping today?" Mum asked.

"That's the last thing in the world I want to do," replied Ted.

"It would be really good if you could help me," said Mum

"Oh, all right then," said Ted reluctantly.

"Then we could go and get a burger, some chips and a milk shake," said Mum.

"Now that's a great idea!" exclaimed Ted.